Rookie
Read-About® Math

Grandfather's Shape Story

WITHDRAWN

By Brian Sargent

Subject Consultant
Chalice Bennett
Elementary Specialist
Martin Luther King Jr. Laboratory School
Evanston, Illinois

Reading Consultant
Cecilia Minden-Cupp, PhD
Former Director, Language and Literacy Program
Harvard Graduate School of Education

Children's Press®
A Division of Scholastic Inc.
New York   Toronto   London   Auckland   Sydney
Mexico City   New Delhi   Hong Kong
Danbury, Connecticut

Designer: Herman Adler Design
The photo on the cover shows a girl and her grandfather talking about shapes.

Library of Congress Cataloging-in-Publication Data

Sargent, Brian, 1969–
  Grandfather's shape story / by Brian Sargent.
     p. cm. — (Rookie read-about math)
  Includes index.
  ISBN-10: 0-516-29919-0 (lib. bdg.)   0-531-16834-4 (pbk.)
  ISBN-13: 978-0-516-29919-8 (lib. bdg.)   978-0-531-16834-9 (pbk.)
  1. Mathematical recreations—Juvenile literature. 2. Tangrams—Juvenile
literature. 3. Shapes—Juvenile literature. 4. Space perception—Juvenile
literature. I. Title. II. Series.
  QA95.S316 2006
  793.74—dc22   2005032732

CHILDREN'S PRESS, and ROOKIE READ-ABOUT®,
and associated logos are trademarks and/or registered trademarks
of Scholastic Library Publishing. SCHOLASTIC and associated logos
are trademarks and/or registered trademarks of Scholastic Inc.

  2 3 4 5 6 7 8 9 10 R 16 15 14 13 12 11 10 09 08 07

My grandfather knows
a special story. He uses
shapes to tell it.

He uses a tangram. A tangram is a puzzle with seven shapes. Together, they form a square.

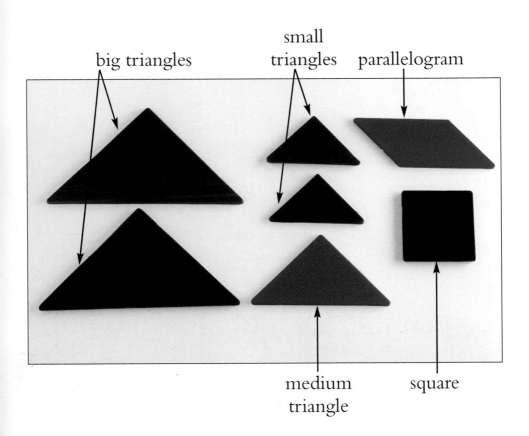

big triangles

small triangles

parallelogram

medium triangle

square

A tangram has two big triangles, one medium triangle, and two small triangles. It also has one square and one parallelogram.

A parallelogram is like a slanted rectangle.

This is my grandfather's story:

In a faraway land, there lived a man. He had little money, and his life was simple.

9

10

One day, the man heard a noise. He heard a voice outside his house. Someone was calling, "Help! Help!"

The man ran outside.
He saw a rooster. He was
surprised when the rooster
said, "Kind sir, will you
help me?"

13

14

"How can I help?" the man asked. "There is a fox looking for me," the rooster said. "If he finds me, he will surely eat me."

The man invited the rooster into his house. He closed the windows. The only light was a single candle.

17

18

As the man poured himself a cup of tea, the rooster spoke. "I am a special rooster. You saved my life and now I will grant you one wish."

The man thought for a
long time. He thought
about wishing for a horse.
It would help him plow
his fields.

21

22

The man thought about wishing for a boat. He could use it to catch fish. He could even travel to other lands.

The man thought about wishing for a wife. He had lived alone for a long time. It would be nice to have someone to love.

25

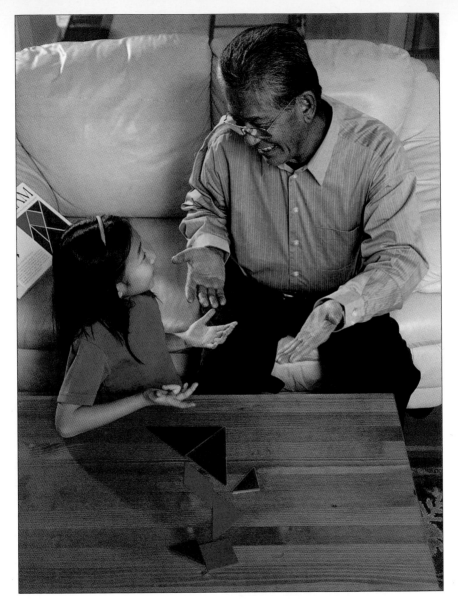

"Make your wish," said
the rooster.

Just then, my grandfather
stopped telling his story.
"Grandfather," I said.
"What did the man
wish for?"

My grandfather pushed the tangram pieces toward me. He smiled. "You choose," he said.

Words You Know

grandfather

parallelogram

square

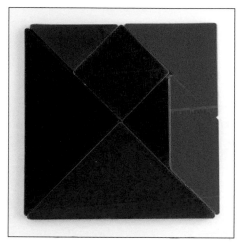

tangram

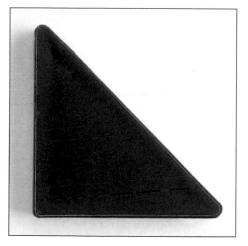

triangle

31

Index

About the Author

Brian Sargent is a middle school math teacher. He lives in Glen Ridge, New Jersey, with his wife, Sharon, and daughters, Kathryn, Lila, and Victoria. He thinks the man wished for a spaceship.

Photo Credits